Stay Safe!

Water Safety

Sue Barraclough

Heinemann
LIBRARY

www.heinemann.co.uk/library
Visit our website to find out more information about Heinemann Library books.

To order:
 Phone 44 (0) 1865 888066
 Send a fax to 44 (0) 1865 314091
 Visit the Heinemann Bookshop at www.heinemann.co.uk/library to browse our
catalogue and order online.

First published in Great Britain by Heinemann Library,
Halley Court, Jordan Hill, Oxford OX2 8EJ, part of Harcourt
Education. Heinemann is a registered trademark of Harcourt
Education Ltd.

Editorial: Diyan Leake and Cassie Mayer
Design: Joanna Hinton-Malivoire
Illustration: Paula Knight
Picture research: Erica Martin
'duction: Duncan Gilbert

'on by Chroma Graphics (Overseas) Ltd
' bound in China by South China

'4 0

British Library Cataloguing in Publication Data
Barraclough, Sue
  Water safety. - (Stay safe!)
  1. Drowning - Prevention - Juvenile literature 2. Aquatic
  sports - Safety measures - Juvenile literature 3. Safety
  education - Juvenile literature
  I. Title
  363.1'23

Acknowledgements
The publishers would like to thank Robin Wilcox for
assistance in the preparation of this book.

Every effort has been made to contact copyright holders
of any material reproduced in this book. Any omissions will
be rectified in subsequent printings if notice is given to the
publishers.

Contents

Swimming and playing in water
is fun.

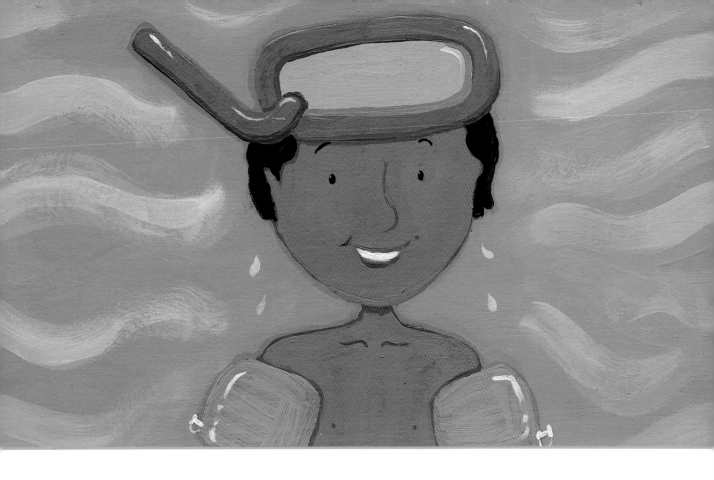

Do you know how to stay safe
in the water?

Never go swimming on your own.

Always make sure a grown-up is watching you.

Never jump and play near water.

Always swim or paddle in a
safe place.

Never swim or paddle in deep or
fast-moving water.

life-guard

Always choose a beach with
a life-guard.

11

Never forget water can be dangerous.

Always use floats if you need them.
Always learn to swim.

Never swim straight after a meal.

Always get out of the water if you
are cold or tired.

Never run or play beside water.

Always be sure there is a
grown-up nearby.

Never get into a boat without
a life-jacket.

Always take care in a boat.
Small boats can tip over.

Always remember these safety rules.

Always take care in or near the water
and you will stay safe.

Water safety rules

- Make sure a grown-up is watching you when you go swimming.
- Check the water before getting in.
- Swim or paddle in a safe place.
- Use floats if you need them.
- Learn to swim.
- Get out of the water if you are cold or tired.
- Be sure there is an adult nearby.
- Take care in boats.

Picture glossary

 **float** something that keeps you from going under the water

 **life-guard** someone who works at a swimming pool or on a beach to help people who are in danger

 **life-jacket** jacket that helps keep you from going under the water

Index

Notes for parents and teachers

Before reading

Ask the children why can it be dangerous near water. Talk about being safe near or in water. Ask the children if they have been to the seaside. What rules did their parents have to keep them safe?

After reading

Moving in water. Put on some suitable music and demonstrate to the children how to move in different ways, such as for paddling (on tiptoe), jumping, wading (big steps), and swimming. Call out the different activities and tell the children to move as you have shown them.

Simon Says. When what "Simon says" is dangerous, the children should put both hands in the air and look sad. When it is safe, they should fold their arms and look happy. "Simon says wear a life-jacket ... go and swim in the sea after a meal ... jump in the water without checking first ... paddle in a safe place ..."

More books to read. Near Water by Ruth Thomson, the Safety First series published by Franklin Watts, *Can You Swim, Jim?* by Kaye Umansky.